About the Author

Luis A. Estable, a poet for more than twenty years, writes in many styles, including songs, children's verses, haikus, and free-style poetry. He has a book of poems out, *31 Felt Poems for My Sweet Sherri*. Thinks that poetry is the most beautiful and compact expression known to man and that criticism is part of the writing life, and to write would be of no worth in the absence of it. It gives an idea of each work quality, though disagreement takes place at times.

RELIGIOUS, TEN SONGS, AND THIRTY SONNETS

Luis A. Estable

RELIGIOUS, TEN SONGS, AND THIRTY SONNETS

Vanguard Press

VANGUARD PAPERBACK

© Copyright 2024
Luis A. Estable

The right of Luis A. Estable to be identified as author of this work has been asserted by him in accordance with the Copyright, Designs and Patents Act 1988.

All Rights Reserved

No reproduction, copy or transmission of this publication may be made without written permission.
No paragraph of this publication may be reproduced, copied or transmitted save with the written permission of the publisher, or in accordance with the provisions of the Copyright Act 1956 (as amended).

Any person who commits any unauthorised act in relation to this publication may be liable to criminal prosecution and civil claims for damages.

A CIP catalogue record for this title is available from the British Library.

ISBN 978-1-83794-686-0

This is a work of fiction. Names, characters, businesses, places, events and incidents are either the products of the author's imagination or used in a fictitious manner. Any resemblance to actual persons, living or dead, or actual events is purely coincidental.

*Vanguard Press is an imprint of
Pegasus Elliot Mackenzie Publishers Ltd.*
www.pegasuspublishers.com

First Published in 2024

**Vanguard Press
Sheraton House Castle Park
Cambridge England**

Printed & Bound in Great Britain

Dedication

To my sweet Sherri, who keeps me trying all I can to improve my poetry, and to those who keep the poetic pen alive each time they buy a book of poetry.

1
SONG # 1

Declare me mad! Declare me mad!
"A world with a living God
Can never be one sad."

But one with zero Deity,
How bad that world would be!
The things permitted that we'd see.

2
SONG # 2

Some talk of the freedom to do.
Some of their right to do as they please.
But then, could you tell the paraphile
Not to pursue the child?

And what if one urinates in the street?
What defense would you have thrown?
To stop the action.

For the sake of sanity,
Or the prevention of chaos
Don't toss the ten commandments!

3
SONG # 3

Yes, we talk about heaven
As being a better place.
Thus, never kill that voice
That talks of the worst of Earth.

If we talk of paradise
Or of eternal life,
It's for we have seen the rise
Of crimes committed upon the Earth.

And we're convinced, and who could doubt,
That better places are.
We've felt that promise within our hearts
And we've seen it with our minds' eyes.

4
SONG # 4

Why not have the woman with the dress
And with the pants the man?
Which clothing belongs to whom
Is in the Bible clarified.

5
SONG # 5

Confusion should never arise
Who is woman and who is male.
There is no book having as a fact

A man can give birth, and a woman can impregnate

And at the birth, God made it thus:
That each with their proper parts.
A girl is born with the vagina,
And the boy has the penis.

6
SONG # 6

To love each other, we're on Earth.
It otherwise can't be!
Absurd it is to think
That other plan had birth.

7
SONG # 7

Not being able to explain what God could be
Is never a reason not to believe!
No one knows the mystery of the seed,
But none questions its existence.

8
SONG # 8

**I know how babies come into the world:
A couple comes together.
But from the womb out to the world,
That magic done, only God knows.**

9
SONG # 9

There is a purpose all divine
In the working out of things.
Still the bird happily sings,
And, too, the rose does grow.

And every man who ever dreamed
Did it with hope and love.
And he who ever looked at the above,
Never failed to imagine a God.

10
SONG # 10

It is understandable
To fail to believe in God.
And even more with those who've suffered most
Or suffering have seen.

But we are creatures with the mind
Not to understand it all.
God is above all things that are,
And we are just mere men.

11
Sonnet # 1

May God, the everlasting and mighty power,
Give me the will to praise Him in my verse.
Yes, this I want to do, lo, every hour.
Oh, how his name I will rehearse, rehearse!
May Him, the grandest One, give me that mean
To serve Him well with this my small poem.
And when I die, in heaven to be seen.
Behind my sins, destroyed all of them.
And may my efforts have somehow the worth
Of them at least one of his glorious feet.
And if this comes to be, yes, what great mirth!
My life on Earth will be one life complete.
With all my force to God, I here do write.
I write to Him with such immense delight.

12
Sonnet # 2

Oh, everlasting flame, I do believe!
Yes, my believing thoughts are ne'er apart.
That I believe in Him and Him conceive
Dwelling in me and touching all my heart.
Yes, God is good and good He does remain.
Though this may be at times you doubt it, yes.
That many earthly minds at times complain.
But his dear heart is good; does love express.
So, then, to God, I drink a glass of wine.
That thanks to Him, I am now well of mind.
And it is small to say that He's divine.
He's everything and adding great and kind.
Oh, God, oh God! The everlasting King!
Oh, God! Oh, God! How humbly this I sing!

13
Sonnet # 3

Truly, the soul goes on, it ne'er does die.
Lo, spirits, lift me to worship my God.
That my eyes look up to the huge, vast sky.
Beyond is God I know; I'm not a sod.
Oh, Jesus Christ did come to save us all.
Yes, glory to his name, I Him proclaim
The prince of peace, the King of kings we call.
All that He is, his everlasting flame.
I am in this, my friends, so born again.
I do believe to heaven I will go.
And to this certainty, I cry some rain.
My happy tears for happier I do grow.
That anything the mouth wishes to say,
The heart does know, and it does God obey.

14
Sonnet # 4

Every seed does give a different tree.
And every animal goes with his like.
And ne'er biology, or botany
Does make mistakes; each with his like does strike.
A man has never given children birth.
And women ne'er have come to shoot some seed.
Nor a rock gets up and dances in mirth.
And when you hit a tree, it does not bleed.
So, then, all reasons are a god is there.
And this to doubt is total foolishness.
So, tell me where there is a mind; yes, where?
That knowing this those other wrongs address.
Yes, everything with its kind it does go.
Never an apple tree, a peach does grow.

15
Sonnet # 5

Our God, who justly does in heaven dwell,
Keep us away from dark and evil sin.
Provide our daily bread and keep us well.
Make all our lives with gladness and hope begin.
Do our temptations stop; don't let us prone.
Advance our mouths, your name so loudly sing.
I know that there in heaven you've a throne.
Your Son besides and you ruling as king.
Give us strength to forgive our enemies.
Guide us, Lord; put us on your Holy Path.
Of your love, please make us his devotees.
And this, this flesh give it a holy bath.
This all He's granted us, what a delight!
Yes, God, this has bestowed; gives us that right.

16
Sonnet # 6

The universal truth God does exist
Is every way we look, in every pond.
How I proclaim that this truth does persist.
That with this truth we will all correspond.
It's there in flowers we with care behold.
And in the birds when they do copulate.
Faces of women that they beauty hold,
And in the spring that all do love not hate.
In every species, they go with their kind.
In every mother where her love firm lives.
In every child on Earth to evil blind.
And in the rose that sweet odor she gives.
A god there is, my world, in all of these.
Heaven will always be and ne'er will freeze.

17
Sonnet # 7

My God, who made the heavens and the Earth.
Who is so now and who will ever be.
Who trusts and wants us to have real mirth
With so much happiness, so bathed in glee.
I pray to you my sins forgive them all.
Give me the power to praise you in my verse.
And let me have what is my highest call:
The verses I write your name as grand rehearse.
And, yes, that glorious day in heaven I
To dwell with angels in my after-life
To be up there with you and say good-bye
To things on Earth that cut like sharp a knife.
That we do have it true that you are good
As true, some trees are made of precious wood.

18
Sonnet # 8

Love your neighbor as you would yourself.
Yes, do good deeds to people, poor or old.
Do battle take with the Devil himself
To push him out until he dies from cold.
Do help the little child, the feeble, and the sick.
Always be patient with the stubborn one.
In recognizing faults, don't be so quick,
Or to condemn a man under the sun.
For God does love you as you really are.
He does not care if you are black or white.
In every one of us He sees a star.
We are his children dear, greatest delight.
By day worship dear God and by night, too.
And be so true to Him; to you He's true.

19
Sonnet # 9

Yes, all the people of this living Earth.
Yes, all its creatures: those who're young, who're old.
Yes, all its mortal beings that had birth
And even granite, stone, and marble cold.
Who made you all and made the sky above?
And all there is, even beyond the doom?
Who made all living things with so much love?
Who gave the rose the best of all perfumes?
It is dear God, the everlasting power.
The One who was, who is, and ever be!
Who knows what comes in every changing hour
Whether you're glad or sad or full of glee.
So, when they call you from among the youth,
To them you say that God is love and truth.

20
Sonnet # 10

I saw a child with happiness, he's playing.
I saw a butterfly so freely flying.
Roses in gardens, flowers were now growing.
And birds on boughs of trees were gladly singing.
I saw a sheep that fresh grass she was eating.
A woman feeding her cute little baby.
Yes, what a day! The sun was brightly shining.
The woman and the child; yes, babe and lady.
And then, I truly knew a god must exist.
To cry some tears, I could not now resist.
And my tears quickly, my cheeks, they so kissed,
And that there is God, I did persist.
Oh, my sweet, happy babe, I say to you,
"There is a God and that has e'er been true!"

21
Sonnet # 11

Don't tell me that I am a foolish man.
And that my mind I need to check, review
With all the given efforts that I can
To see if my untrue can have some true.
That a huge fantasy is in my brain
And like an idiot big, I go and go
And sit under the light and see false rain.
When I do think of you, I sadder grow.
No faith in God, the one deceived is you,
Not to believe that a god must exist.
This is no news but old, ever seen new.
All things are made by God; do not resist!
Both dark and light to God, they are the same.
I do praise what God is, not merely name.

22
Sonnet # 12

To all recording time I here do pen
With much love that I do want to show.
I do not doubt but firmly say, "Amen."
With jollity, I'm wet and happier, I grow.
For I do know, I'll go with brightest face.
Look at dear heaven, for He is up there.
With a gleam in my eyes, I feel the place
Where joyous souls do live; his love they share.
He is a mighty God, and He's forever
And wants our lives to be delightful scene.
And we should truly live like sisters and brothers,
And all those evil thoughts to wash them clean.
This certainty that God's in all that's good.
I am immensely glad, knock upon wood.

23
Sonnet # 13

My sins I do confess and pray to thee.
Do from my mind erase the bad I've done.
Make me rejoice; give me tranquility!
And cleanse my thoughts; give me a glowing sun.
To you, I come and ask for open arms.
Receive me as I am; I know you will.
For this, I pray to you with no alarms.
Though I do know from sin that I am ill.
The knowledge that I keep, your good does show.
Your everlasting love for us on Earth.
So, I believe in you and trumpets blow.
I do respond with tears, your enormous worth.
How like a father you appear to me!
How like a child I say, "Oh, happy me!"

24
Sonnet # 14

My terrifying thoughts: *Oh, God, I fear!*
My spirits feel ashamed for I did sin.
Habitual act I feel bad to adhere.
One day you may punish my sinful skin.
Please, God; yes, lift my soul, my human soul.
So, I can purify and clear my mind.
The correct achievement of desired goal.
You are the greatest One, so good and kind!
I come to you so you can give me strength.
My nerves are not of steel, and I do cry.
Give me the might, and I will go the length.
And then, I will live life so apple pie.
That you are both: The Merciful, The Good.
How could I sin? Oh, God; yes, how I could?

25
Sonnet # 15

Yes, how I do worship my God so dear!
I worship Him in a daily praying feast.
And to this faithful feast I do adhere
All kinds of energies; ne'er have them ceased.
That the Lord being both female and male,
What a glorious state! He loves us all!
Yes, to praise his name, I'll never fail.
And when I don't feel well, on Him I call.
Heaven belongs to Him; He gave us Earth.
So, to respect that gift, let's come and love.
He is our father and sees us with worth.
Though we from Earth can't see Him there above.
My daily prayer I do; yes, this I do.
Worshiping, praising Him I do, so true.

26
Sonnet # 16

In everything we see, it's there, it's there
A present God. Believe it, it's no mistake.
And I will surely never ever dare,
Yes, try to change what truly is no fake.
It is in flowers and things we behold.
The tree, the woman, and the baby's face.
And I by older people have been told,
A face with wrinkles—that's your given grace.
And with his glory all of this He made.
We should be brothers, side by side to dwell.
Our daily sins, our faults were ever paid
When Jesus came so we won't go to hell.
Worship my God with all that I do find,
I hourly do for He's immensely kind.

27
Sonnet # 17

How good to live when if you come to err,
In heaven you will have it all so well.
Oh, double easy life! And it is fair.
And best of all, you will not go to hell.
For God is good and kind we should behave
For with eternal life, we will be blessed.
Hark! Nothing says we are a worthless slave.
By God, we're all considered his high best.
If this be error for the mind so speaks,
We have the heart to say this here is true.
The mind is silly and sometimes it leaks.
The heart is serious and does love anew.
Oh, paradise is living, yes, above.
Being with God and having all his love.

28
Sonnet # 18

My spirits are so high; I like who I am.
My blood is clean, a substance I could kiss.
Representation of the Lord's sweet lamb.
When I consume myself, I am, yes, his.
My heart does beat, does beat. I have a drum.
And in my mind, there is nothing of hell.
And in this case, I do happy I become.
My life's a rose and sweet the given smell.
Oh, God! The Mighty Spirit from above!
He looks at us and knows our every need.
And it's for free we have his daily love.
That who believes in Him, he will succeed.
So good is mighty God that daily He
Wants us to have of life the best to be.

29
Sonnet # 19

That I believe; please, don't call me a fool.
I know there's a God who sees it all.
You learn what's taught; that they do spread at school.
But what is right can never ever fall.
You don't believe! Allow me to say this:
You are naïve who doubts this possible.
Your foolishness brings you to an abyss
Ne'er to get out; that is most plausible.
There is the rain and, too, there was the cloud.
Who made the rain before there was a cloud?
I overpower and I'm not disavowed.
And this I say, my voice put to the loud.
All things on Earth give notice to my call.
"There is a God, and this is seen in all.

30
Sonnet # 20

I worship God the High; He is our source.
With all I can to Him, my life I give.
Tremendous numbers of a fine discourse,
My mind declares this how I now do live.
I worship Him, the One who made it all.
My spirits rise as if from ashes some fire
Making decisive my so-human call.
My certain knowledge that I do acquire.
It's with delight that I worship; I do,
A God so good, my love does grow so bright.
He brings to me a scene so clear, so true.
The consequence is good; my life is light.
And like a child I rise and say, "Amen!"
In God I do believe, and should all men.

31
Sonnet # 21

Oh, why do you hate Jesus? Tell me, man!
Yes, why have you ne'er seen your dark, ill feeling?
That Jesus came according to God's plan,
God's children free from a hell they were living.
That any flesh that goes to a hellish cross
Deserves respect through action all alone.
But the dear blood of Christ no drops of loss.
Those who succeed do happily bemoan.
And, yes, dear Jesus is of God the Son.
And you in keeping, so worship his name.
There are men everywhere under the sun
Who sank in sin and He removed that blame.
To Jesus give to Him what is his due.
He did suffer so glad; to us He's true.

32
Sonnet # 22

I did wake up one pretty summer morn',
And looked around, the leaves looking so green.
And in this picture that did quite adorn
I was perplexed as if for first it's seen.
I saw the birds upon the boughs did sing.
I watched the sheep eating so peacefully.
Though I am not, I felt I was a king.
Dozens of songs I sang so merrily.
And I again looked up, this time the sun,
And made no doubt that a god must exist.
And in this happiness a song begun,
"God made all living things." I did persist.
This moment precious was and precious we
By dear God to be loved, and what a glee!

33
Sonnet # 23

In all this world and all the men in it,
In all the breathing mouths and beating hearts.
I make my care; my care is definite,
That bathes in honesty and with truth starts.
In all their scope and in their daily lives
That put a show of so much daily fun.
That makes so glad our hearts and much sweet gives
To live in comfort under the moon, the sun.
Believe there is a God in heaven dwells.
Who was and is and ever always will.
And He his love for Him does not compel,
But does allow that it should be our will.
That He is everlasting with the ever.
And not to exist He will come never ever.

34
Sonnet # 24

Don't call my firm belief that it is dumb.
Don't call me a fool for I surely believe.
I have so many songs that I do hum.
Worship dear God: He does gladly receive.
I am in my belief so truly wet.
This is my God, who is and ever will.
And in my circumstance, you can so bet,
That I will do my best to help the ill.
Look at the child when he does have a smile,
And ask if chance just put it firmly there.
Nor Mister Devil can truly compile,
Outdo the hand of God to say I dare.
That all the universe, the Earth below
Created both by God and so did grow.

35
Sonnet # 25

Yes, in my sleep I dreamt the perfect dream.
That up in heaven we with God were all.
My heart was filled with joy, I thought supreme,
And in my head my happiness ne'er small.
To dwell with angels, us forever and ever
And walk the silver streets with pearly light.
And for this good never depart, yes, never.
The best of best of worlds; yes, sweet delight!
And see at last his presence like a kid,
And showered by his bountiful soft love
That He much has, and never has it hid.
That wonderful abode, that life above.
This to my mind appears a thing so kind!
To hear the deaf and then, to see the blind.

36
Sonnet # 26

No! I say yes to that! And no, to this:
To cursing God! And yes, to praising Him!
That when I praise dear God: Oh, what a bliss!
When curse I give, in life I badly swim.
The everlasting Master! The ever-Knower!
Who moves my soul, and I cry like a child
Who has a father, and who has a mother
They both love him and about him are wild.
So, my contentment is where God does dwell.
The precious day when I with God belong
To leave this life that surely leads to hell
And live a life with nothing ever wrong.
And in that state to stay forevermore.
Nothing to fight, or to be truly sore.

37
Sonnet # 27

God: in the smile of a little child.
God: in the faces of that one called female.
God: in the lamb that is so meek and mild.
God: when she cries her cry the nightingale.
God: in the working hands of that who's male.
God: in the flowers of summer and the spring.
God: in the mother her job does not fail.
God: in those who go from nothing to a king.
God; in every person and his human soul.
God: in every place where there's a thing.
God: in those people that the poor console.
God: in the infant to his mom does cling.
God: forever and forevermore.
God: who cures the deaf, the blind… the sore.

38
Sonnet # 28

That you are fat or have not pretty a face.
God does love no fault; keep that in mind.
And sees in you a soul of ever grace,
And by his loving actions, He's so kind.
That you're deformed in ways so rarely seen.
God of your body cares; you are his child.
I know this well for in his care have been.
He takes care of the lamb; to Him he's mild.
Oh, dear my God! You are so good, you are!
That in your eyes I am a human star!
And it's not in the minimum bizarre
That you are close to us, though you are far.
To all humanity, open your eyes!
Your lives down here, dear God does recognize.

39
Sonnet # 29

His resounding name that ne'er will fade.
The One who knows it all and all He made.
Give glory to that name; don't be afraid.
Substantiating substance it has aid.
The power limitless, the knowledge supreme.
Good, sweet, and kind, and caring for us all.
To exactitude, my mind does now high scream.
To see this true, my senses do not fall.
Oh, God! Yes, Mighty God, so grand you are!
That in your sight I am a precious star.
No quarrel I with you; you hold the bar.
Tremendous happiness comes from afar.
Your scope is above all, your healing love.
I on my knees do fall; look at the above.

40
Sonnet # 30

If you do good, God's love is heaven-sent.
Oh, how sweet this whole Earth, my friends, could be!
Accommodating big, no accident!
It is a fact I've seen so affirmative.
If each would love his neighbor as himself,
What loving lives we could so firmly live.
And on this Mother Earth, upon herself
Our lives would be those lives so positive.
And all would be so precious at its best.
So, let us live as God wants us to do,
And make awareness that we are so blessed
As roses their perfume, perfume so true.
My brother, I am you; you, brother, me.
And this confirmed what great tranquility!

www.ingramcontent.com/pod-product-compliance
Lightning Source LLC
LaVergne TN
LVHW041816111224
798846LV00006B/212